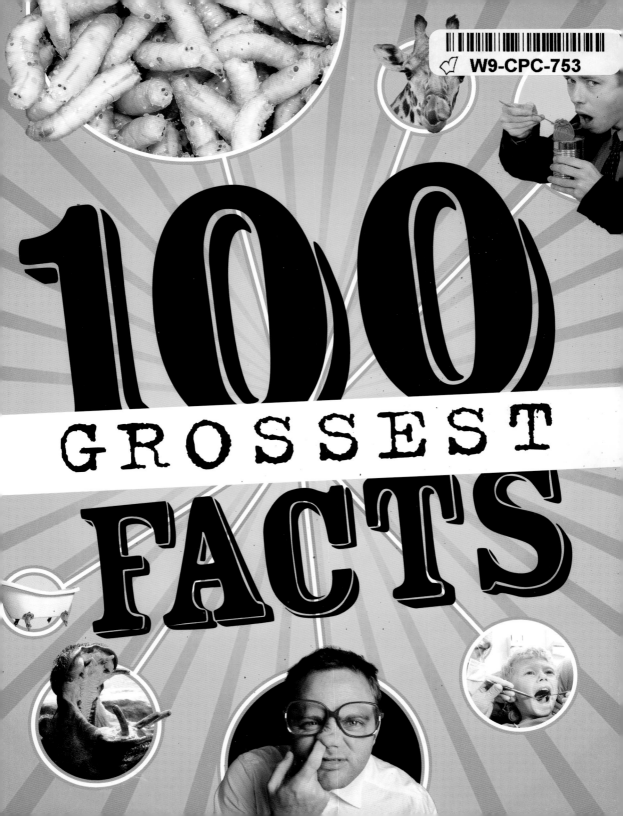

100 GROSSEST FACTS

Editorial and Design: Dynamo Ltd and Fineline
QEB Project Editor: Alexandra Koken

First published in the United States in 2013 by
QEB Publishing, Inc.
3 Wrigley, Suite A,
Irvine, CA 92618

www.qed-publishing.co.uk

A CIP record for this book is available from the Library of Congress.

ISBN 978 1 60992 616 8

Printed in China

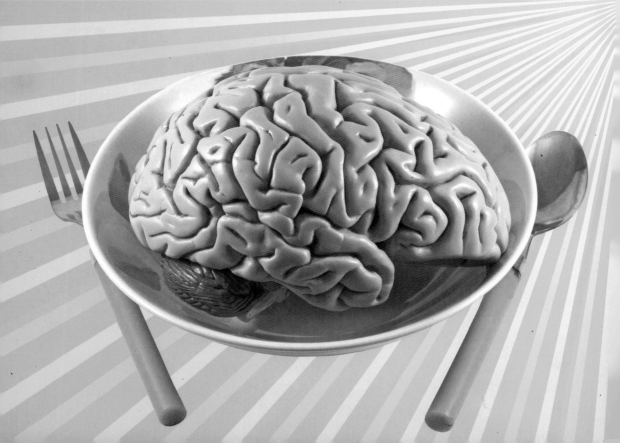

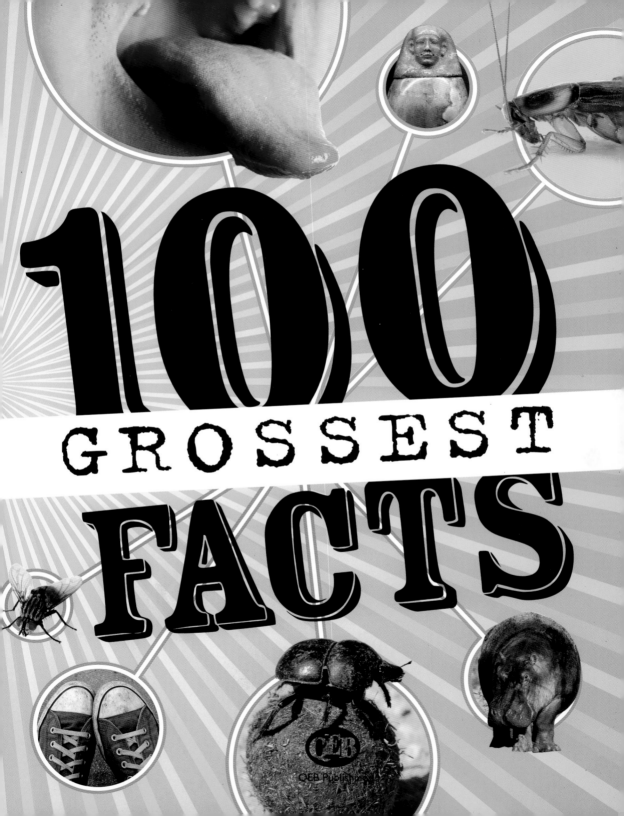

100 GROSSEST FACTS

QEB Publishing

CONTENTS

King Henry VIII's most important servant had to wipe the monarch's bottom.

In the time of the Tudors, the kings and queens who ruled England between 1485 and 1603, the Groom of the Stool was an important position among a monarch's servants.

FAST FACT!

Desperate for a male heir to the throne, King Henry VIII married six different wives in the hope that one of them would bear him a son.

The person who held this job looked after the monarch when they went to the bathroom. It sounds like a terrible task, but those who took the role were often told secrets and had great influence. Some were even given lands and titles as a reward.

Hippos sweat a sticky red fluid that looks like blood.

To keep their unique skin moist when they are out of the water, hippos secrete a substance from their pores. This is called "blood sweat" because of the way it looks. Yuck! It's actually quite helpful to the animals as it protects them from sunburn and even infections.

FAST FACT!

Hippos are very dangerous and kill more people in Africa each year than lions.

A mattress, pillow, and blanket can house 100,000 dust mites.

FAST FACT!

Dust mites don't drink, but can absorb moisture from the air. Most male dust mites live for less than 20 days.

Scientists believe that thousands upon thousands of mites can exist in a home, feasting on flakes of dead skin and other matter, and helping to cause allergies.

The house dust mite is a tiny creature, rarely larger than 0.04 centimeters long with an almost see-through body. This makes them hard to spot with the naked eye, but that doesn't mean they're not present in YOUR home.

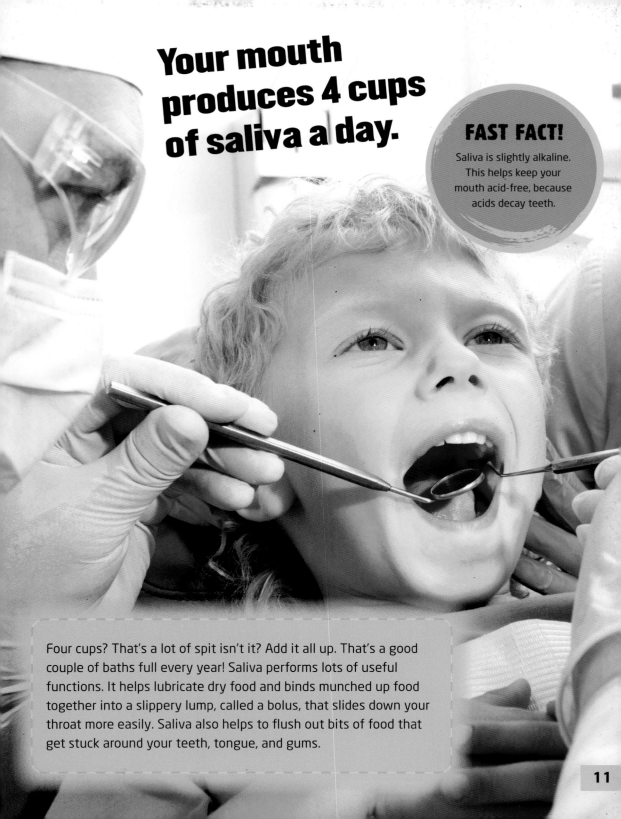

Your mouth produces 4 cups of saliva a day.

FAST FACT!

Saliva is slightly alkaline. This helps keep your mouth acid-free, because acids decay teeth.

Four cups? That's a lot of spit isn't it? Add it all up. That's a good couple of baths full every year! Saliva performs lots of useful functions. It helps lubricate dry food and binds munched up food together into a slippery lump, called a bolus, that slides down your throat more easily. Saliva also helps to flush out bits of food that get stuck around your teeth, tongue, and gums.

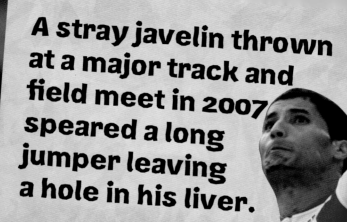

A stray javelin thrown at a major track and field meet in 2007 speared a long jumper leaving a hole in his liver.

FAST FACT!

At the 1996 Olympics, U.S. shot putter John Godina accidentally hit team partner Randy Barnes in the back with a shot. Luckily, Barnes wasn't injured.

The accident occurred at an IAAF Golden League track and field meet held in Rome's Olympic Stadium. The javelin event and long jump competition were being held at the same time.

The javelin that hit French long jumper, Salim Sdiri was thrown accidentally off target by Finland's Tero Pitkamaki. Luckily, Sdiri recovered, and in 2009 he made his longest ever jump— a distance of 27.6 feet.

The first President had dentures made from hippo teeth.

FAST FACT!

George Washington was president for two terms, so for a total of eight years. During this time the United States capital changed from New York City to Philadelphia.

George Washington started losing his teeth in his twenties, and by the time he was sworn in as President of the United States he only had one left! Washington wore a number of different sets of false teeth throughout his life. Several sets made by his dentist Dr. John Greenwood featured plates made of gold and teeth carved from those of a hippopotamus.

Before she became famous, Whoopi Goldberg worked as a make-up artist for corpses.

Actress, comedian, and talk show host Whoopi Goldberg won an Oscar in 1990 for her role in the film *Ghost*. But long before she became famous, Whoopi, who was born Caryn Elaine Johnson, had some strange jobs.

FAST FACT!

Whoopi Goldberg has appeared in or provided her voice for more than 150 movies. She is the second African American actress to have won an Oscar.

To make ends meet while playing small parts on Broadway, Whoopi took a course as a beautician and found work applying make-up to dead bodies in a funeral parlor.

Clothes in Ancient Rome were cleaned using vats of wee.

In ancient Rome, woolen clothes were soaked in large wooden vats to be cleaned. Some of these were full of wee and slaves had the unpleasant job of wading into the vats to tread and work the liquid through the cloth. Urine contains ammonia, a chemical that actually helped clean the cloth. This became such a common practice that one Roman emperor, Vespasian (9–79 CE), began to tax pee from public urinals which was sold to the fullers for cleaning.

FAST FACT!

In 1917, modern artist Marcel Duchamp displayed a urinal on its back as a work of art entitled *Fountain*.

When making a mummy, the ancient Egyptians pulled the brain out through the nose using a hook.

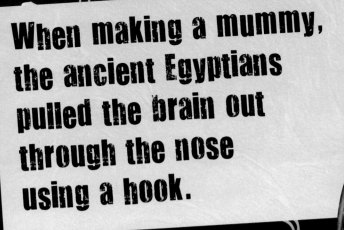

Mummification in ancient Egypt was a long, complicated process. One of the first stages was to remove the dead person's brain. A hook was thrust up the nose into the skull to access the brain. It was then teased and pulled out through the nostrils.

Historians believe that the brain was often thrown away, but other organs removed from the body, such as the stomach and lungs, were preserved in special containers called canopic jars.

FAST FACT!

Many ancient Egyptian mummies were prepared by packing the body with an absorbent salt called natron.

Carrots were once purple.

Carrots were first grown for food in the Middle East and India more than 1,000 years ago. They were smaller and less sweet than modern carrots, and usually purple, though some were pale yellow. In the 1600s, Dutch farmers crossed strains of carrots to grow plumper, juicier varieties that were orange. In 2007, a British gardener grew the world's longest carrot measuring 19 feet.

FAST FACT!

China grows more carrots than any other country in the world. Around 45% of the world's 32 million tons of carrots are grown there.

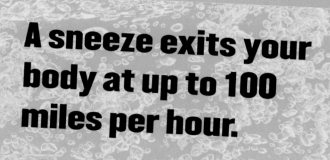

A sneeze exits your body at up to 100 miles per hour.

A sneeze is your body's way of getting rid of something that is irritating the lining of your nose, such as dust or pollen. Nerve signals cause you to take a deep breath, which is then expelled from your nose and mouth at a great speed. The mucus (snot) from a sneeze can travel 5 feet away, which is why covering your nostrils with a tissue or hankie is a good idea. Did you know that you always close your eyes at the moment you sneeze?

A competition is held to find the child with the stinkiest sneakers.

Sponsored by Odor-Eaters, the Rotten Sneaker Contest is open for children aged 7 to 17 who possess seriously smelly sneakers. Pity the poor judges who have to sniff and decide which foul footwear is the worst of all. The winner gets a Golden Sneaker trophy, $2,500, and their sneakers are enshrined in the Hall of Fumes in Vermont.

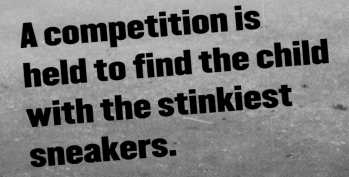

The average person passes gas between seven and fifteen times a day.

FAST FACT!

How much gas you produce and how often you tend to release it is determined by a range of factors, including what you have eaten.

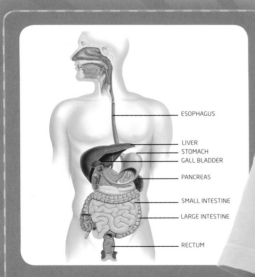

ESOPHAGUS

LIVER
STOMACH
GALL BLADDER

PANCREAS

SMALL INTESTINE

LARGE INTESTINE

RECTUM

Your digestive system breaks down nutrients from the food you eat, providing energy to fuel your body, and for growth and repair. Your digestive system also makes between one half to 3 pints of excess gas per day.

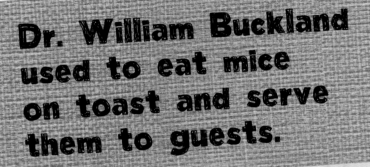

Dr. William Buckland used to eat mice on toast and serve them to guests.

Buckland (1784-1856) was a pioneering geologist and one of the first to describe the dinosaur species *Megalosaurus*. He also vowed to eat a sample of every creature on Earth—and he literally meant every creature. Over the years he ate an elephant's trunk, panther, kangaroo, rhinoceros pie, and horse's tongue. He also enjoyed the sliced head of a cooked porpoise and mice on hot, buttered toast.

FAST FACT!

Buckland's least favorite foods were bluebottle flies and moles!

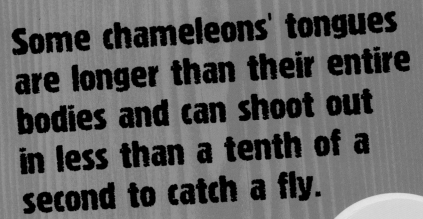

Some chameleons' tongues are longer than their entire bodies and can shoot out in less than a tenth of a second to catch a fly.

When not in use, the tongue is wrapped up inside the chameleon's mouth. In an explosive movement, it fires out and stretches to its full length to catch its prey.

There are more than 150 species of chameleon. They vary in length from less than 1 inch to up to 4 feet. Some have outrageously long tongues. Panther chameleons, for example, have tongues up to one and a half times the length of their own body.

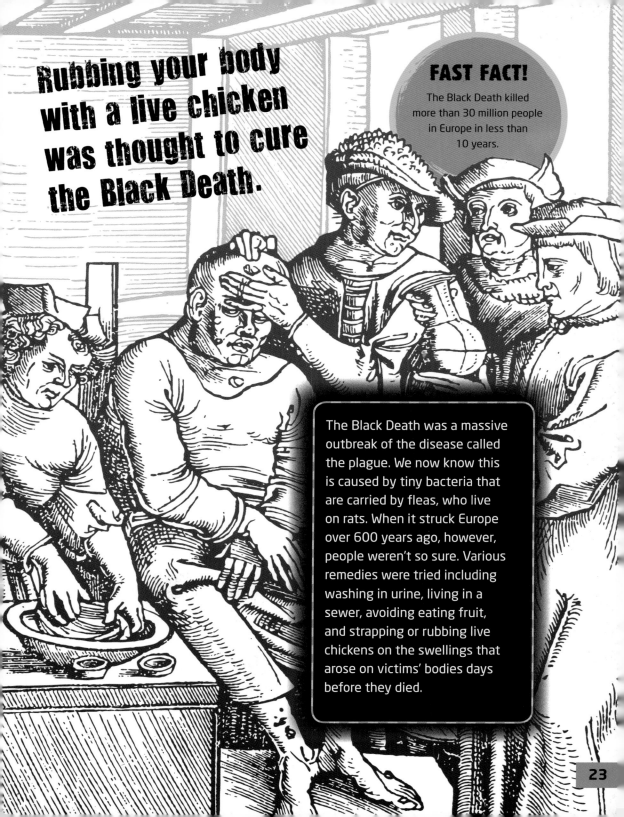

Rubbing your body with a live chicken was thought to cure the Black Death.

The Black Death was a massive outbreak of the disease called the plague. We now know this is caused by tiny bacteria that are carried by fleas, who live on rats. When it struck Europe over 600 years ago, however, people weren't so sure. Various remedies were tried including washing in urine, living in a sewer, avoiding eating fruit, and strapping or rubbing live chickens on the swellings that arose on victims' bodies days before they died.

Butterflies drink their own urine.

FAST FACT!

Reindeer also lick up urine to gain salts in icy environments. Some reindeer herders in Siberia go for a wee to attract their reindeer to where they are standing!

This shocking fact may be a surprise, but butterflies do this to survive. While they sip nectar from flowers as their main food source, they also need to obtain certain salts and minerals for their bodies to be healthy. These are contained in their urine, so after they've weed, they'll suck it back in through a long sucking tube that acts as their mouth.

John F. Kennedy towed an injured man 4 miles in the water using his teeth.

FAST FACT!

Elected as President of the United States in 1960, John F. Kennedy became the youngest President at 43 years old. He was tragically shot and killed in November 1963.

During World War II, John F. Kennedy (who later became President) was in command of a torpedo boat, PT-109, when it was severely damaged by a Japanese destroyer.

The survivors had to swim almost 4 miles in the South Pacific to reach an island where they were later rescued. Kennedy, who had been on the Harvard University varsity swim team, towed an injured crewman, Patrick McMahon, by clenching his teeth on a life jacket strap.

The gulper eel can swallow prey many times larger than itself.

Living as deep as a mile underwater, the gulper eel has a gigantic mouth that has a long hinge so that it can open really, really wide to swallow a fish or other sea creature much larger than itself. The eel's lower jaw has a pouch like a pelican and its stomach can stretch to accommodate its meal. Despite its weird shape, scientists believe that it mostly uses its mouth as a big sieve to filter out small marine creatures like shrimp.

FAST FACT!

The deep sea viperfish has teeth so large they don't fit into its mouth. Instead they sit menacingly outside, ready to bite its next victim.

The biggest centipede is 12 inches long and bites!

FAST FACT!

Prehistoric insects were even bigger due to higher oxygen content in the air. They could grow up to 10 feet long!

Scolopendra centipedes can be more than 12 inches long—the length of a school ruler. Most of these creepy crawlies are nocturnal and hunt for other insects and mice at night. Using their large fangs they bite their prey again and again, injecting them with venom with every bite. Even though these massive critters can't kill a human, their bite is definitely painful!

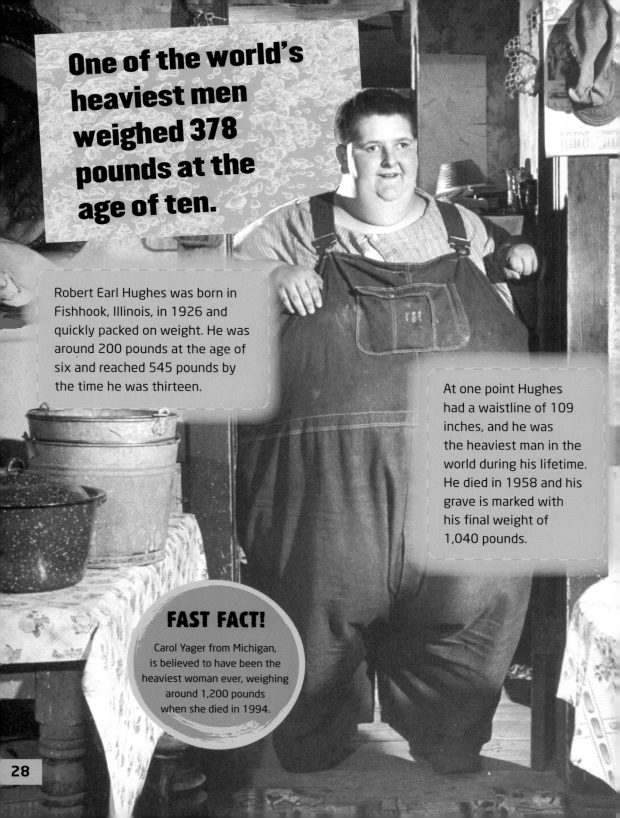

One of the world's heaviest men weighed 378 pounds at the age of ten.

Robert Earl Hughes was born in Fishhook, Illinois, in 1926 and quickly packed on weight. He was around 200 pounds at the age of six and reached 545 pounds by the time he was thirteen.

At one point Hughes had a waistline of 109 inches, and he was the heaviest man in the world during his lifetime. He died in 1958 and his grave is marked with his final weight of 1,040 pounds.

FAST FACT!

Carol Yager from Michigan, is believed to have been the heaviest woman ever, weighing around 1,200 pounds when she died in 1994.

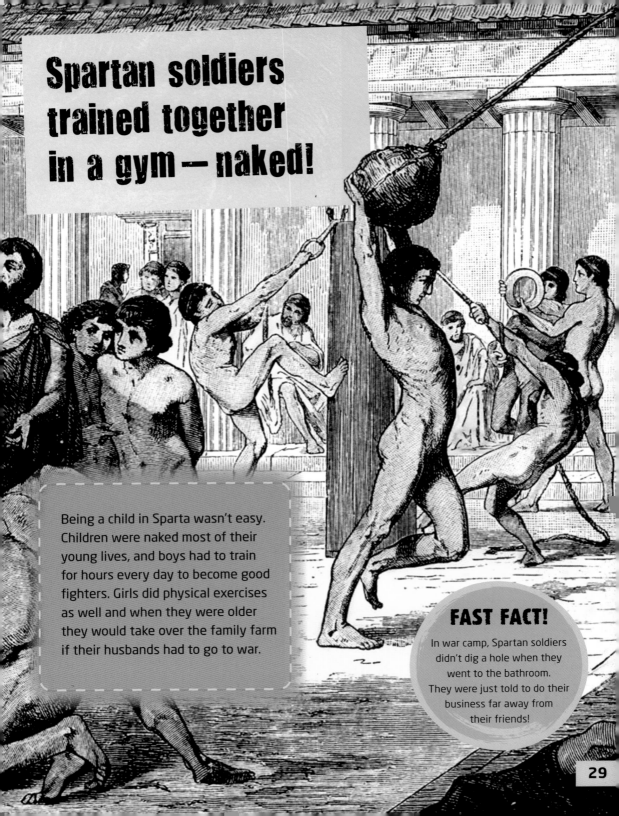

Spartan soldiers trained together in a gym — naked!

Being a child in Sparta wasn't easy. Children were naked most of their young lives, and boys had to train for hours every day to become good fighters. Girls did physical exercises as well and when they were older they would take over the family farm if their husbands had to go to war.

FAST FACT!

In war camp, Spartan soldiers didn't dig a hole when they went to the bathroom. They were just told to do their business far away from their friends!

Each of your feet can produce more than a cup of sweat a day. Ewww!

Ever pulled your sneakers and socks off after a hard day's play and nearly fainted because of the stink? It's all to do with the sweat that your body expels from tiny sweat glands through openings in the skin called pores. Sweating gets rid of waste materials your body no longer needs, and also helps to cool you down.

FAST FACT!

On average, men sweat more than women. Someone working physically hard in a hot climate can sweat as much as 4 gallons a day.

Your feet have more sweat glands than other parts of your body–around 250,000 of them– which is why your feet sweat a lot when you're hot.

In 2001, it rained red rain for a month in Kerala, India.

You'll definitely want an umbrella if you come across one of these weird weather sensations—and it's been happening for centuries! Scientists still aren't sure whether the rain turns red from algae or dust from the desert, but these disgusting drops can be as thick and bright red as real blood. It wouldn't actually harm you, but it could certainly dye your clothes pink. Who would want to look like they'd showered in blood?

Bladderworts are carnivorous plants that can capture creatures in just a hundredth of a second.

Some plants get nutrients by capturing and digesting small creatures. Found in ponds, bladderworts consume the larvae of insects and small crustaceans, which they capture using small trap doors. When potential prey gets close, it touches trigger hairs around the trap door, causing it to open and shut at speeds too fast for the human eye to see, and trapping the creature inside.

FAST FACT!

Most carnivorous plants capture insects, but occasionally frogs and even small birds may get caught by larger plants.

Scientists created a mouse that has a human ear growing on its back.

The so-called Vacanti Mouse, named after Dr. Charles Vacanti, was created at the University of Massachusetts in 1997. The ear mold was made from special fibers and injected into the back of a mouse, where it grew to be the size of a human ear. The technique of this experiment was invented to regrow ears and noses for people who were born without them or lost theirs in an accident.

Gary Turner's skin is so stretchy that he can make his face disappear!

Gary Turner, also known as "Stretch", currently holds the record for world's stretchiest skin! Due to a rare genetic disorder, his skin is so elastic that he can pull the skin from his neck completely over his lower jaw. Some of his other tricks include stretching out his belly into a table so that it can hold three large drinks, and using heavy bulldog clips to pull his skin down into different shapes.

The bamboo rat lives in large bamboo forests. Every 48-50 years the forests sprout large numbers of flowers and seeds. This is believed to be responsible for a huge increase in rat numbers that invade surrounding farmland, eating almost anything they come across. More than 2.6 million rats were caught by people in a part of the Ayeyarwaddy Delta in India, between June and September 2009.

Every 50 years or so, massive plagues of rats infest parts of India.

FAST FACT!

The Gambian Pouched Rat can grow up to 3 feet long and weigh 6.5 pounds.

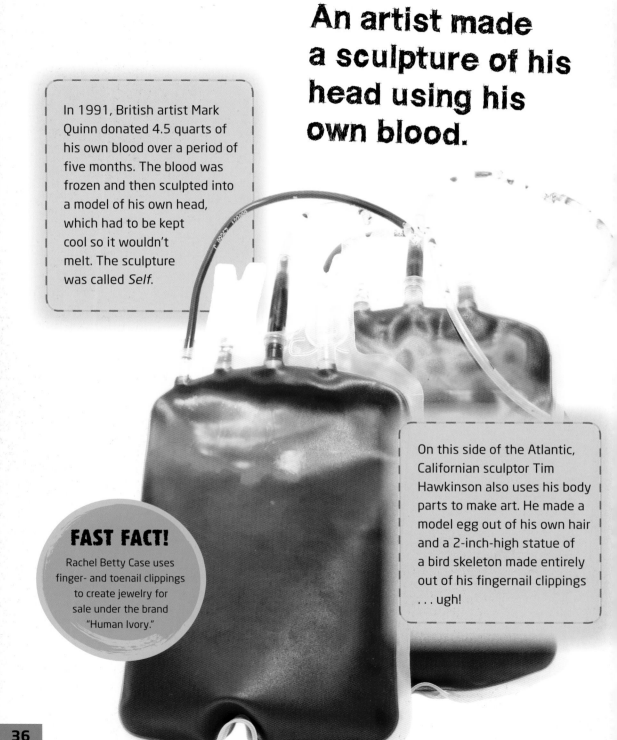

An artist made a sculpture of his head using his own blood.

In 1991, British artist Mark Quinn donated 4.5 quarts of his own blood over a period of five months. The blood was frozen and then sculpted into a model of his own head, which had to be kept cool so it wouldn't melt. The sculpture was called *Self*.

On this side of the Atlantic, Californian sculptor Tim Hawkinson also uses his body parts to make art. He made a model egg out of his own hair and a 2-inch-high statue of a bird skeleton made entirely out of his fingernail clippings . . . ugh!

FAST FACT!

Rachel Betty Case uses finger- and toenail clippings to create jewelry for sale under the brand "Human Ivory."

Nicholas Cage ate a real cockroach on film.

Actor Nicholas Cage starred in the 1989 movie, *Vampire's Kiss*. During the film he goes increasingly insane and in one scene he catches and eats a live cockroach. This wasn't a stunt.

Cage had to eat a living cockroach. Actually, he had to eat two as the movie's director, Robert Bierman, insisted on filming two takes of the scene.

FAST FACT!

Nicholas Cage's uncle is film director Francis Ford Coppola. Cage changed his surname so that he would be respected more for his talent than for his famous name.

A starfish has two stomachs!

FAST FACT!

Although they live underwater, starfish—also known as sea stars—are not actually a type of fish.

Unlike humans and most other animals, a starfish has two stomachs—the cardiac stomach and the pyloric stomach. To help digest its food and prey, a starfish pushes the cardiac stomach out of its mouth to engulf it more easily. It then sucks the cardiac stomach back in and passes the food over to the pyloric stomach, where the food is digested further.

A woman ate 45 hot dogs in just 10 minutes.

Every year, Nathan's Hot Dog Eating Contest is held on Coney Island. It is so popular that 40,000 fans attend and it is televised on sports TV channels. In 2012, Sonya Thomas won the women's event by gulping down 45 complete hot dogs in buns. The men's 2012 champion, six-time winner Joey Chestnut, managed a whopping 68 hot dogs. Do not try these challenges at home. Sonya and Joey trained hard for years to do this!

Lee Redmond holds the record for the world's longest fingernails!

By not clipping her fingernails for over 30 years, Utah resident Lee Redmond grew them to an impressive 3 foot long and set a record for the world's longest fingernails. Spanning almost five times the length of Redmond herself, the unusual nails made a number of TV appearances and featured in *National Enquirer* tabloid, who kept track of their progress every few years.

FAST FACT!

Following a car accident in 2009, Lee Redmond survived but her famous fingernails were broken.

Thousands of rats live in an Indian temple.

The Karni Mata temple in Deshnok, in the Indian region of Rajasthan, is home to as many as 20,000 rats that are looked after and worshipped by hundreds of human followers. These animals are considered sacred by followers of the Hindu religion and many Hindus travel long distances to see them.

Astronauts wear underpants filled with liquid coolant.

Space is VERY cold, but astronauts working outside a spacecraft in large, sealed spacesuits can overheat, so their ingenious high-tech underwear is designed to keep them cool. Around 280 feet of plastic tubing are fitted inside stretchy material to make up these cool undergarments. Heat transfers from the body into water in the tubes, and is piped away to a refrigeration unit inside the astronaut's backpack. There the water is cooled and then recirculated around the underwear.

There are huge lumps of fat in London's sewer system called "fat bergs."

In 2010, enough fat bergs were removed from London's sewer system to fill nine double decker buses, and that was only from underneath one small area! The fat bergs are created by people pouring cooking fats down their drains, which then clog up the sewage system under the streets. Gross!

FAST FACT!

This clean-up action removed 1,000 tons of fat, and was only said to last a couple of weeks before it all got clogged up again.

44% of adults in a survey admit they eat their own boogers.

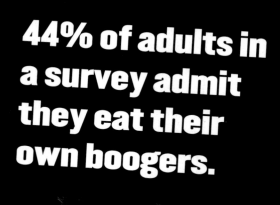

Now, that's gross! It's also childish of adults when you consider how often they scold children for doing the same thing. Boogers are just dried mucus from the inside of your nose and contain dead disease-fighting cells called phagocytes. Food science writer, Stefan Gates, surveyed adults for his 2005 book, *Gastronaut*, and found that almost half ate the contents of their nostrils.

It takes around 70,000 crushed beetles to make 1 pound of carmine dye.

Carmine dye gives a strong red color. It was once used in artists' paints and in cloth and fabric dyes. Today, carmine is still used in many countries as a colorant in foods such as processed meats and cakes, as well as to color cosmetics. Carmine dye is made from crushed cochineal beetles, and Peru is the biggest producer in the world.

FAST FACT!

Tyrian purple was a dye extracted from sea snails, and was highly prized by the ancient Greeks and Romans. It took thousands of snails to dye clothes.

The durian fruit is banned from some places in parts of Asia because of its nasty smell.

FAST FACT!

Other things that are illegal in Singapore include chewing gum, sleeping in public, and not flushing the toilet!

Durian trees grow in Southeast Asia to heights of more than 80 feet. Their fruit is covered in a thorny husk and can grow up to 12 inches long and 6 inches wide. When opened to reveal the fleshy fruit inside, a powerful smell hits your nostrils.

Some people consider the durian fruit the "king of fruits," while others think it smells of manure and rotting vegetables. Its smell can be so strong that it has been banned from public transport in Singapore. It has also been banned from some hotels, aircraft cabins, offices, and hospitals.

You may have mites living on your eyelashes.

FAST FACT!

An eyelash mite's maximum walking speed is about 1 inch per hour.

These tiny creatures grow to about one third of a millimeter long and can only be seen under a microscope. They live on eyelashes where they eat old skin cells and the natural oil produced by the hair follicle in the skin. They have eight short, stubby legs and the older you are, the more likely you are to have them. They are found on about one third of children's and teenagers' lashes and about two thirds of elderly people.

A hippopotamus can open its mouth wide enough to fit a 4-foot child inside!

A hippo's mouth is enormous! Its mouth can hinge wide open at an angle of 150 degrees, displaying teeth up to 20 inches long, and leaving enough space inside for a small child.

After the elephant and the white rhinoceros, the hippopotamus is the third largest land animal, and can weigh as much as 3.175 tons. It moves easily in water, and can reach speeds of 18 to 25 miles per hour over short distances on land.

FAST FACT!

The hide of a hippo is very thick and heavy and can weigh 1,100 pounds. To keep their temperature down, hippos bathe in mud and water regularly.

Albert Einstein's brain was removed from his body after he died, and kept for scientific research!

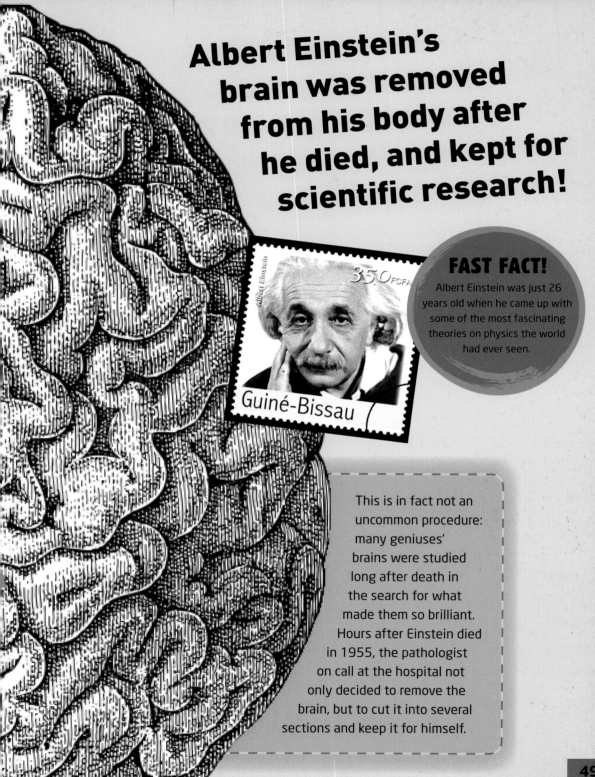

Albert Einstein

35.0 FCFA

Guiné-Bissau

FAST FACT!

Albert Einstein was just 26 years old when he came up with some of the most fascinating theories on physics the world had ever seen.

This is in fact not an uncommon procedure: many geniuses' brains were studied long after death in the search for what made them so brilliant. Hours after Einstein died in 1955, the pathologist on call at the hospital not only decided to remove the brain, but to cut it into several sections and keep it for himself.

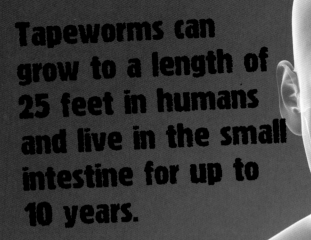

Tapeworms can grow to a length of 25 feet in humans and live in the small intestine for up to 10 years.

FAST FACT!

There are more than 1,000 species of tapeworms. Three species have been found living inside horses in North America.

Tapeworm is the common name given to a number of species of flatworms. These develop inside other creatures after their eggs or tiny young, called larvae, are accidentally eaten. A tapeworm living in a human has a series of hooks around its head, which it uses to attach itself to the intestine, so that it can draw in nutrients from the person's digested food.

If left untreated, a tapeworm can live as long as 10 YEARS inside its human host. Gross!

People in Africa eat mopane worms as a snack.

FAST FACT!

Over 1,000 species of insects are eaten by people. In a restaurant in Vancouver, Canada, you can order cricket pizza, a doughy base sprinkled with roasted crickets.

That's right, especially in Zimbabwe and some other southern African nations. Mopane worms are not worms at all. They are giant caterpillars of the emperor moth that feed on leaves of the mopane tree, hence their nickname. Once caught, their insides are squeezed out. Then they are either left to dry out so they can be eaten as a crispy snack or they are fried and covered in a spicy sauce.

A giraffe can clean its nose and grasp branches with its 20-inch tongue.

Giraffes are the tallest animals on land, with an incredible 6.5 foot neck, which allows them to reach tree shoots and leaves that are out of reach for other animals.

Their long tongues can grab and pull branches toward their mouth. An adult giraffe eats up to 175 pounds of foliage a day.

House flies go to the bathroom almost every 4.5 minutes!

Yes, in the same time it takes us to brush our teeth or listen to a song, one of our favourite household pests, the house fly, passes its waste. As house flies are well known for being major transporters of viruses and bacteria, too many of them could cause health issues, so it's important for us to clean out our garbage and keep them well away from food.

53

More than 1,800 pairs of hobbit feet were made and used in *The Lord of the Rings* movies.

FAST FACT!

Actor Viggo Mortensen bonded so much with his character's horse on the set of *The Lord of the Rings* that he bought it after filming had finished.

The Lord of the Rings film trilogy, directed by Peter Jackson, was one of the most ambitious film productions ever, with a cast of thousands and vast amounts of make-up, special effects, and props required. Designers and seamstresses produced over 19,000 costumes, while 48,000 pieces of armor and 10,000 arrows were created for filming.

The world's most expensive coffee, kopi luwak, is made in Indonesia from wild animal droppings.

The Asian Palm Civet lives in southern Asia and eats the fleshy fruit surrounding the coffee beans. The bean travels through the cat's digestive system where chemicals cause it to lose some of its bitter flavor. Around a day and a half after being eaten, it passes out of the Civet's other end.

Kopi luwak farmers collect the Civet droppings, wash off the beans, and sell them for as much as $595 per pound.

FAST FACT!

Some people in Malaysia keep Civets as pets!

A Frenchman once ate an entire Cessna 150 light aircraft.

Yes, you read that right. Michel Lotito was born in 1950, and earned the nickname Monsieur Mangetout for his amazing and foolish (don't try it at home) ability to consume just about anything–from bicycles to a chopped up pair of skis.

N53059

In the Venezuelan city of Caracas, between 1978 and 1980, Lotito dined on a Cessna light aircraft, washing down each small, chopped up part of the plane with mineral water and oil.

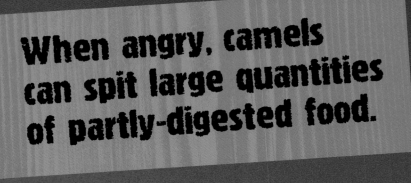

When angry, camels can spit large quantities of partly-digested food.

If a camel is angry or distressed, it brings up partly-digested food from its stomach back into its mouth. This gloopy soup contains food, saliva, and some stomach acid, and smells really bad. The camel then flings this stinking liquid at its target, which can be anything from another camel, an animal it considers a threat, or even a human that annoys it. Just make sure you get out of the way fast enough!

FAST FACT!

Certain spitting spiders spit sticky venom at their prey to stop it from moving.

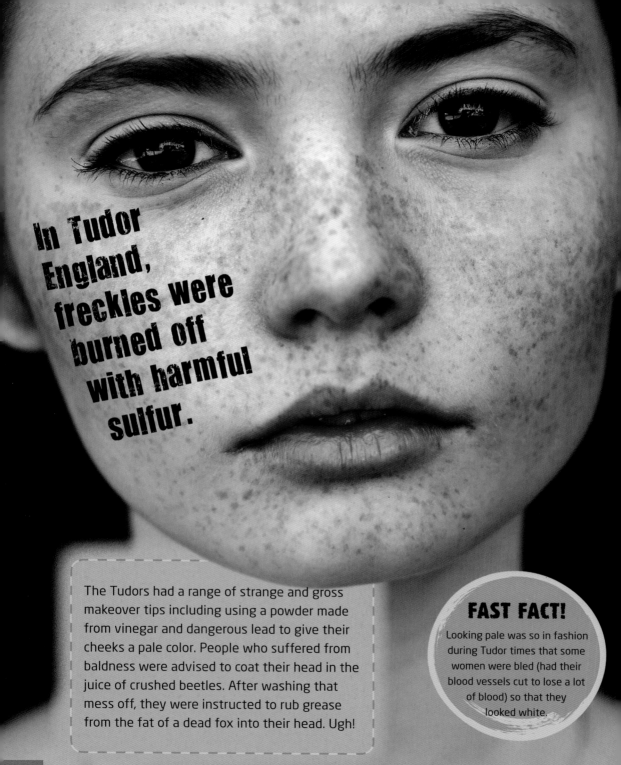

In Tudor England, freckles were burned off with harmful sulfur.

The Tudors had a range of strange and gross makeover tips including using a powder made from vinegar and dangerous lead to give their cheeks a pale color. People who suffered from baldness were advised to coat their head in the juice of crushed beetles. After washing that mess off, they were instructed to rub grease from the fat of a dead fox into their head. Ugh!

FAST FACT!

Looking pale was so in fashion during Tudor times that some women were bled (had their blood vessels cut to lose a lot of blood) so that they looked white.

Dogs eat their own vomit!

FAST FACT!

As well as eating their own vomit to hide their traces, dogs also eat their own waste!

Yes, believe it or not, dogs often eat their own vomit. In the wild, dogs live in packs, so eating their own vomit helps them to cover their tracks and stops other dogs or predators from finding them. Sometimes, dogs also regurgitate their food to feed their puppies. Although pet dogs are domesticated, many still have the instinct to provide food for their young and so haven't completely lost this habit.

Niek Vermeulen from the Netherlands has a collection of over 6,000 different airsickness bags (empty, of course)!

FAST FACT!

Niek Vermeulen's massive collection of airsickness bags has come from more than 1,000 airlines in more than 160 different countries.

It is strange what some people will collect. This Dutchman had a bet with a friend to see who could collect the most of an object. While flying, the idea to collect sick bags from airlines came to him.

Among the giant collection is his most prized exhibit –an airsickness bag from the NASA Space Shuttle *Columbia* which had traveled for 16 days in space.

After use close by folding · Nach Gebrauch schließen durch Falten
Après usage fermer par plier

Sickness bag
Spuckbeutel
Sac vomitoire
Sickness bag
Spuckbeutel
Sac vomitoire
Sickness bag
Spuckbeutel
Sac vomitoire
Sickness bag
Spuckbeutel
Sac vomitoire

Sickness bag
Spuckbeutel
Sac vomitoire
Sickness bag
Spuckbeutel
Sac vomitoire
Sickness bag
Spuckbeutel
Sac vomitoire

The Vikings used their urine to help start fires.

Apart from being serious warriors, the Vikings were pretty clever at using the substances they found around them. They would gather up a special type of fungus–like touchwood or oak agaric– which grows on trees, slice it and then place it in a pot full of urine that they would boil for several days. Urine contains sodium nitrate, which reacted with the fungus. The resulting material could be lit and left to smolder without properly burning for a long time. This meant an easy source of fire could be transported, by ship or over land.

Casu Marzu is an Italian cheese eaten while full of living fly maggots.

This stinky cheese is a definite contender for not only the world's most disgusting cheese, but also the grossest food. Made from sheep's milk on the island of Sardinia, it is left outside so that cheese flies (Piophila casei) can lay their eggs inside it.

Hundreds of maggots hatch from the eggs and nibble away, producing chemicals that give the cheese a really strong taste that can burn the tongue.

In the crypts of Palermo, Italy, mummies stare down at you, often with their hair and skin still intact!

FAST FACT!

Some of the skeletons have lost teeth and small bones over the years. Imagine accidentally stepping on a centuries-old finger! Yuck!

In 1599 a monk was embalmed and buried in a crypt under the monastery where he spent his life—and months later the monks discovered his body had simply dried out and became mummified! Local people got wind of this ghoulish affair and asked to be buried in the mysterious crypt . . . and now 8,000 mummies line its walls!

One cure for epilepsy in seventeenth-century England involved consuming human brains.

All sorts of strange cures for epilepsy were suggested throughout the ages including eating raw liver and consuming belladonna: a poisonous plant. English doctor John French concocted a seriously brainy remedy for epilepsy. You were to take the brains of a young man who had died a violent death, grind them down, and leave them in wine and horse dung for months before taking a sip. Gross, gross, gross!

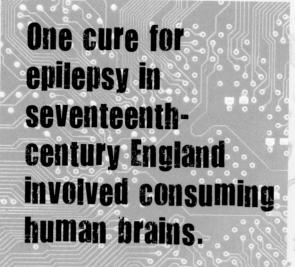

FAST FACT!

King Charles II of England used the "King's drops" when he had a headache—they were made from powdered human skull mixed in alcohol.

When a comic book writer died, his ashes were used to print a comic he had written.

Mark Gruenwald was a talented writer and artist who worked on many famous Marvel comic books including the *Captain America* stories. When he died in 1996, his body was cremated and his ashes were mixed with the ink used to reprint *Squadron Supreme*, a comic he had written in 1985.

FAST FACT!

His friends did not actually believe Mark was dead, because they knew he was such a joker!

The Colossal Squid has the world's biggest eye— bigger than a soccer ball.

Not much is known about the mysterious Colossal Squid, which can dive to great depths in the ocean—up to 1.2 miles. Only a few specimens of this creature have been studied, but scientists believe it can grow to a length of over 45 feet.

A specimen captured off the coast of Antarctica had an eyeball measuring more than 10 inches in diameter. In comparison, a full-sized soccer ball measures just 9 inches across.

FAST FACT!

One reason for the squid's large eye is so it can spot predators, such as the sperm whale, from far away, helping it to escape from harm.

Mehmet Yilmaz can squirt milk from his eye!

In 2004, Turkish man Mehmet Yilmaz set a new Guinness World Record for squirting milk from his eye into a coffee cup from over 6 feet away. He achieved this by snorting the milk through his nose before squirting it out across a table! However, not everyone can do this. While swimming in a pool a few years earlier, Yilmaz noticed that bubbles were coming out of his left eye. The strange bubbles were the result of a pressure leak inside his eyelids.

A special fish eaten in Japan has to be carefully prepared, because parts of its body contain enough poison to kill 30 people.

The fearsome fish in question is fugu (also known as puffer fish). It is a delicacy in Japan, but chefs have to be specially licensed to prepare and sell it. The fish contains tetrodotoxin, a poison more lethal than cyanide. As little as 0.0009 ounces of tetrodotoxin can kill a person.

FAST FACT!

The liver is the most deadly part of the fish, and has been banned in Japanese restaurants since 1984.

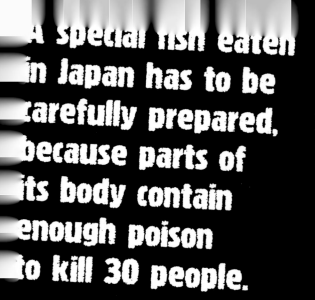

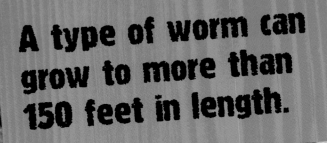

A type of worm can grow to more than 150 feet in length.

FAST FACT!

Bootlace worms can stretch up to several times their natural length.

Bootlace worms are found around the coasts of the United Kingdom and northern Europe. They can be found in tidal pools, underneath boulders, and on muddy shores, and can grow to enormous lengths. Specimens measuring 150 feet—that's longer than a blue whale—have been found, making it the longest known creature on Earth.

Some people have jobs as dog and cat food testers.

Seriously. These people are pet food gourmets who are employed by pet food companies to check that their new recipes will be rated as purrfect by cats and tail-waggingly good by dogs. Pet food testers open sample tins, take a big forkful and make notes on the taste, texture, and aroma. A thumbs-up may see the new flavor go into stores. Most testers chew gum and gargle mouthwash after a tasting session to avoid having dog breath!

FAST FACT!

Chew Chew, a restaurant purely for dogs, opened in Sydney, Australia, in 2010. Beef steak and lamb bones were on the menu for pampered pooches.

Some wealthy ancient Romans were real gluttons. They put on feasts or banquets for important guests that lasted hours and involved many, many courses. Among the dishes would have been rare and exotic delicacies including elephant's trunk, dolphin meatballs, boiled parrots, peacock, and camel. Soups sometimes included sea urchins or jellyfish while the tongues of birds from the tiny lark to the larger flamingo were also eaten.

Roman feasts included flamingos, stuffed dormice, and ostrich brains.

FAST FACT!

An elaborate Roman feast featured three courses (appetiser, main, and dessert), silver cups and utensils, and even entertainment!

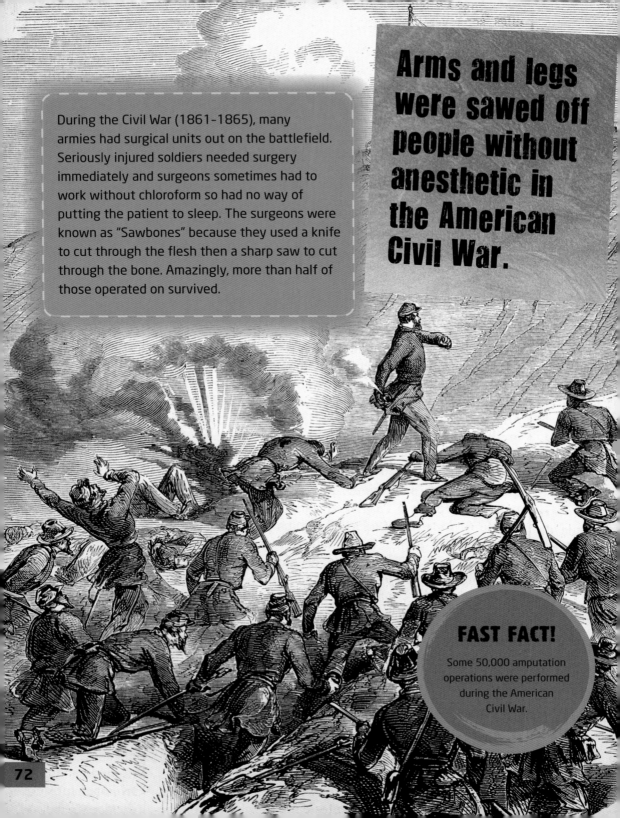

During the Civil War (1861–1865), many armies had surgical units out on the battlefield. Seriously injured soldiers needed surgery immediately and surgeons sometimes had to work without chloroform so had no way of putting the patient to sleep. The surgeons were known as "Sawbones" because they used a knife to cut through the flesh then a sharp saw to cut through the bone. Amazingly, more than half of those operated on survived.

Arms and legs were sawed off people without anesthetic in the American Civil War.

FAST FACT!

Some 50,000 amputation operations were performed during the American Civil War.

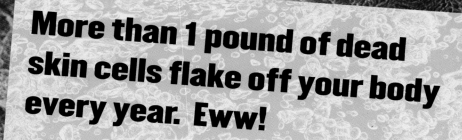

More than 1 pound of dead skin cells flake off your body every year. Eww!

Your body continuously generates new skin cells. At the same time, dead skin cells are flaking off all the time. As you read this, many hundreds of skin cells will fall off your body. It is estimated that dead skin accounts for as much as 900 tons of dust in the Earth's atmosphere.

FAST FACT!

An average square centimeter of skin contains 150 nerve endings to help your sense of touch, as well as detecting temperature and pain.

A Japanese Emperor's favorite food was boiled or fried wasp larvae.

Emperor Hirohito, like a number of people in Japan, loved hachi-no-ko. This traditional dish features wasp larvae taken freshly from wasp nests, cooked in sugar and soy sauce to give them a crumbly texture and then served on a bed of rice. In Mexico some Mexicans will eat a tortilla filled with guacamole, tomato salsa, and escamoles. Sounds fine, until you realize escamoles are ant eggs!

King Louis XIV of France is said to have only taken three baths during his entire life.

King Louis was a renowned soap dodger. His physicians advised him against baths thinking that a layer of dirt and grime would protect him from germs and disease. Russian ambassadors at the stinky king's court reported that he smelled like a wild animal.

FAST FACT!

It wasn't just Kings. Queen Isabella of Castile admitted she only took two baths during her life.

Maybe it ran in the family as Louis' grandfather Henry IV smelled so bad that when she first met him, Marie de Medici is said to have fainted because of the stench. Despite this, she became his wife!

A huge pizza baked in South Africa had a diameter of 122.7 feet.

Weighing over 26,800 pounds, the pizza was prepared in 1990 outside a supermarket in Norwood, South Africa. A staggering 9,918 pounds of flour, 1,984 pounds of tomato puree, and 3,968 pounds of cheese were used. Other giant foods include a 2,998 gallon ice cream float and a banana split that was 4.5 miles long!

FAST FACT!

Did you know Italy's favorite frozen pizza is produced by a German company–just outside of London?

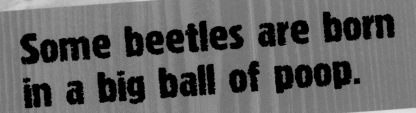

Some beetles are born in a big ball of poop.

Many dung beetles live off the poop of herbivores such as cows. They gather together dung and roll it into a ball . . . and a big ball at that. It's often more than 40 times bigger than the actual beetle. Beetles roll their ball of dung to a safe place, sometimes burying it as a food store or using it as a nest, known as a brooding ball. Female dung beetles lay their eggs in the ball so that the babies are born in the middle of a food source.

FAST FACT!

Swallowtail caterpillars disguise themselves as bird droppings so that other creatures don't eat them.

Stutterers once had parts of their tongues cut out as a cure.

During the eighteenth and nineteenth centuries, some doctors in Europe performed surgery to cut out parts of the tongue in an attempt to stop stuttering. It must have been excruciatingly painful and there was no evidence that it ever cured a stutter.

FAST FACT!

Some famous people who stutter include actress Marilyn Monroe, golf player Tiger Woods, and author Lewis Carroll. Luckily all of them had better treatments than this one!

Butterflies taste food with their feet.

As crazy as it sounds, it's true. Butterflies have taste receptors on their feet or to be more scientific, their tarsi—the name given to the last segments of their legs.

FAST FACT!

Monarch butterflies travel around 2,000 miles from the Gulf of Mexico to the Great Lakes region in the spring.

These taste receptors detect different chemicals. It is believed that female butterflies use them to track down sweet nectar to take in as their food, and to figure out if a plant is a suitable place on which to lay their eggs.

150,000 tomatoes are thrown in an hour during a huge food fight in Buñol, Spain.

La Tomatina is a festival that grew out of a food fight with vegetables during a parade in 1945. Today, thousands of participants and spectators wait for a loud alarm at 11 a.m. on the last Wednesday in August.

Then, the madness begins. Up to 89,950 pounds of tomatoes are brought in on carts, pulped, and thrown in a frenzy for 60 minutes. Afterward the town's fire engines hose down the square and the participants.

A Pacific island made a fortune from bird droppings.

FAST FACT!

The white part of bird poop is the equivalent of a human's pee. Birds need to retain water more than humans, and so for birds it comes out as a white paste.

The tiny island of Nauru was covered in guano—the droppings of seabirds. This was mined because it is rich in phosphate, which makes it a very good fertilizer for growing crops. For a time in the mid-twentieth century, Nauru became rich from this mining, which generated millions of dollars, but when the guano ran out, the island was left mostly deforested and with little soil.

The world's largest hamburger weighed 777 pounds.

The mega-burger was made at the Alameda Country Fair in California, in 2011, with pieces sold off at 99 cents each. It featured over 600 pounds of beef cooked into a giant patty and served on a bun weighing a staggering 110 pounds, along with 20 pounds of onions, 30 pounds of lettuce, and 12 pounds of pickles! The whole burger contained 1,375,000 calories.

A man once earned 20,000 French francs a week by blowing gas out of his bottom.

Incredible but true! Joseph Pujol (1857–1945) was a baker by trade, but he started to give public performances of his unique talent. Pujol would suck in and blow out gas from his bottom and was even able to extinguish candles on stage with his gusts.

The talented baker was also able to imitate musical instruments with his behind. He became a highly paid star act at the Moulin Rouge theater in Paris from 1892 onward. On one occasion, the King of Belgium went to see his act.

The first animals to survive in outer space are called tardigrades or "water bears."

FAST FACT!

Some tardigrades are able to survive without water for a staggering ten years.

These tiny creatures—the largest is just half an inch long—can survive large doses of radiation that would kill other animals. In 2007, a batch of tardigrades were sent into space. Most survived without oxygen or water for ten days.

An adult dairy cow is able to produce more than 18 tons of manure in a year.

FAST FACT!

Before milking machines were invented in 1894, farmers could only milk about 6 cows per hour. Today, farmers use machines to milk over 100 cows per hour.

A large dairy cow weighing over 1,300 pounds drinks the equivalent of a bathtub full of water and eats between 30 and 60 pounds of food each day.

As a result, a cow can produce more than 100 pounds of wet manure in 24 hours, as well as large quantities of gas which it expels from its bottom and also by belching.

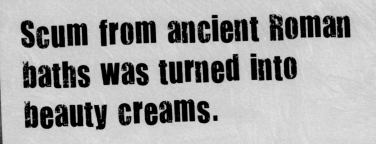

Scum from ancient Roman baths was turned into beauty creams.

FAST FACT!

Another Roman beauty cream recipe included honey, vinegar, fat from chickens, and crocodile dung.

The Romans loved their public baths and instead of soap they used olive oil, which was rubbed onto them by slaves. The oil, dirt, and gunk was scraped off the body with a blade called a strigil. Most of this horrid scum was thrown away but some enterprising Roman businessmen collected it from baths, mixed it with herbs, and sold it as beauty cream!

A man set a world record by eating 36 cockroaches in one minute.

You're probably familiar with speed-eating record-holders such as Canadian Pat Donahue who guzzled 91 pickled onions in 68 seconds. Ken Edwards' record set on TV in 2001 is a whole different level of disgusting. The retired rat catcher from England ate 36 cockroaches in 60 seconds. Did we mention the cockroaches were still alive? Yuck, yuck, and double-yuck!

The horned lizard can squirt blood from its eyes.

FAST FACT!

The skunk can produce a gross-smelling scent that can scare off predators as far as 12 feet away.

Found in North America, where they mostly dine on ants, horned lizards have several lines of defence from predators such as snakes, coyotes, and foxes. Firstly, their skins are camouflaged so that they can blend in to the local surroundings. Secondly, if threatened close up, they puff up their bodies and stick up their spines to look much bigger and more fearsome. Last but definitely not least, if still under attack, they can burst small blood vessels in and around their eyes squirting blood distances of up to 5 feet.

Earwax is mostly dead skin bound together with oil, wax, and dirt.

Did you know your ear has sweat glands? These produce a waxy substance called cerumen. This mixes with dead skin cells that flake off as well as any dust or dirt present and an oily substance called sebum. As disgusting as the mixture sounds, it performs a valuable job protecting your delicate inner ear from fungus, bacteria, and even insects that might crawl in.

FAST FACT!

While we're on the subject of ears, Anthony Victor from Madurai, India, holds the world record for the longest ear hair—a whopping 7 inches long!

The giant petrel is also known as a 'stinker' due to the foul-smelling oil that it vomits at predators!

FAST FACT!
While petrels use their oil as a defence mechanism in the animal world, humans have also used it for medicinal purposes, rubbing it into tired muscles.

The Northern Fulmar, or seabird, is a distinctive species of petrel with a very unique habit. It has a well-earned reputation for being a 'stinker' due to the revolting odour of the oil it fires at other animals when in danger. The oil can stick to the feathers of birds, which damages their ability to stay waterproof and can later cause them to drown.

There's a championship for throwing cow pats as far as possible.

Held in the town of Beaver, Ohio, every year since 1970, the World Cow Chip Throwing Championship sees contestants hurl a dried cow pat as far as they can. Contestants are allowed to shape their pat as it dries into a flying disc-like shape. The world record for distance thrown was actually set a long time ago in 1981 at a different event, the Mountain Festival in Tehachapi, California. Steve Urner managed to hurl a cow pat a staggering distance of 266 feet.

Ground-up dinosaur bone is used as medicine in parts of China.

FAST FACT!

A large *Brontosaurus* dinosaur would have generated thousands of quarts of gas per day from its vegetarian diet.

Villagers in China's Henan Province have dug up thousands of dinosaur bones. One dollar would buy you 1.5 pounds of "terrible dragon bones." They are used in traditional Chinese medicine, ground up into a powder that is then used in dry form or mixed with liquid to make a soup. It is used to treat broken human bones, leg cramps, and dizzy spells.

A heavily polluted fog hit London in 1952 and killed 12,000 people.

In early December 1952, a mysterious fog hit London. At the time, most Londoners kept warm by burning coal in their homes. Coal was also used in factories and vehicles burned leaded gasoline without any pollution controls. All of this mixed with the fog to create a heavy smog that damaged people's lungs. Visibility was also reduced to just a few feet, which caused a rise in car accidents.

FAST FACT!

In 2005, thousands of frogs fell in a freak storm onto the Serbian town of Odzaci.

An eleven-year-old once attempted to break the record for most live snails on a face!

FAST FACT!

They may be small, but a single garden snail can have up to 430 babies in a year!

Keen to set a new world record for most live snails on a face for 10 seconds, eleven-year-old Fin Keleher from Sandy, Utah, made the headlines in 2009 when he allowed an impressive 43 of the slimy creatures to be placed upon him. A total of 87 snails had been gathered from neighbours' backyards for the attempt, but only those that remained on Fin's face for the full 10 seconds counted.

When slime eels are taken out of the water and handled, they drip with sheets of slime!

FAST FACT!

Long and flexible, this unusual eel can tie itself into a knot in the water and then pass the knot down its body to wipe away any slime.

The Atlantic Hagfish, more commonly known as the slime eel, earned its name due to the gruesome slime that drips from its body when removed from the water. In the animal world, this sticky slime actually serves a very useful purpose to the eel, as it can help to protect it from predators such as fish by clogging up their gills and suffocating them.

Live maggots are sometimes used to eat dead human flesh off living patients!

FAST FACT!

Other bizarre healing methods include applying leeches to suck a patient's blood where it has become clotted.

When a nasty wound can't heal itself properly and the flesh starts to rot, doctors can apply a rather disgusting treatment by putting live maggots on the wound. The sterile maggots are bred especially for this purpose and only eat the dead flesh, leaving the wound clean and ready to heal. Ugh!

Body snatchers used to dig up dead bodies from graveyards.

In the past, scientists, surgeons, and medical schools were eager to practice their skills and learn more about the human body. The demand for dead bodies led some people to become body snatchers, taking bodies from fresh graves in church cemeteries and delivering them to doctors or medical schools in return for money. In 1830 and 1831, police caught seven bodysnatching gangs in London alone.

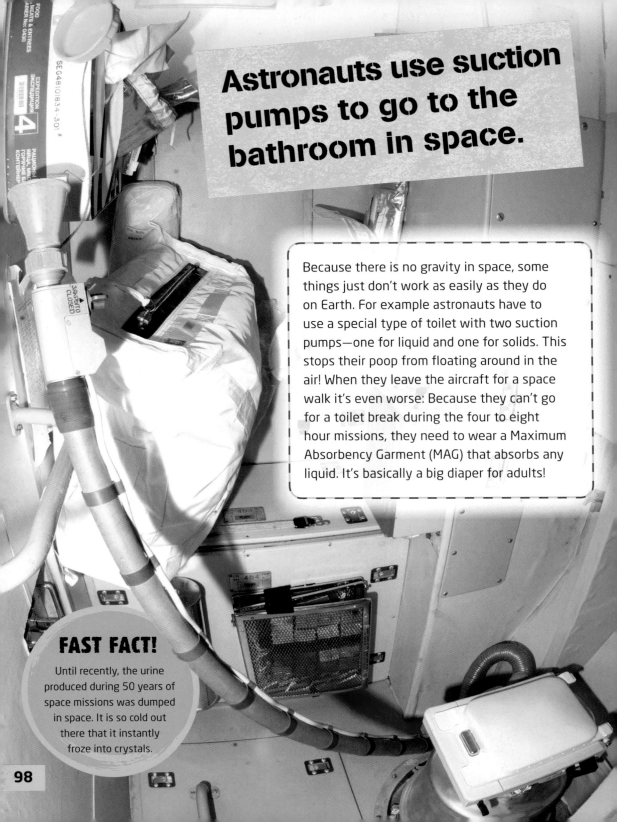

Astronauts use suction pumps to go to the bathroom in space.

Because there is no gravity in space, some things just don't work as easily as they do on Earth. For example astronauts have to use a special type of toilet with two suction pumps—one for liquid and one for solids. This stops their poop from floating around in the air! When they leave the aircraft for a space walk it's even worse: Because they can't go for a toilet break during the four to eight hour missions, they need to wear a Maximum Absorbency Garment (MAG) that absorbs any liquid. It's basically a big diaper for adults!

FAST FACT!

Until recently, the urine produced during 50 years of space missions was dumped in space. It is so cold out there that it instantly froze into crystals.

If you were a catfish, you could taste a slice of pizza just by sitting on it.

FAST FACT!

There are 2,200 species of catfish and they make up eight percent of the total number of fishes.

That's right! Catfish have amazing senses, including taste buds that cover most of their body, including their whiskers, fins, stomach, back, and tail. A catfish just 6 inches long has around 250,000 taste buds on its body. Certain rare types of catfish can grow up to 6.5 feet long. You can see why they are sometimes called "swimming tongues"...

A baby's first poop is black and gooey!

A baby's first poop is thick, black, and sticky because it's been sitting inside the baby's intestines for weeks before they were born. Babies can get diaper rashes from wet diapers, can projectile vomit, and need to be "burped" after meals—but on the whole they can be cute, too.

FAST FACT!

When they are born, babies have no kneecaps. They grow later on!

The King of England's body exploded.

William the Conqueror was from Normandy, France, but took control of England following his invasion in 1066. In 1087 while in Normandy he died and his body was to be buried in Caen, in today's France. William died of a major infection in his intestines, and gases from the infection caused his already large body to bloat even more. When people tried to squeeze his body into a stone coffin, it burst, filling the air with a disgusting smell. Urgh!

FAST FACT!

Famous classical composer Joseph Haydn had his head stolen after his burial in 1809. It wasn't reburied with the rest of him for over 140 years.

When a pharaoh or rich person in ancient Egypt died, embalmers prepared his or her body for the afterlife. As part of this process all organs except the heart were removed and kept in special, canopic jars: one for each of the following—the liver, intestines, lungs, and stomach. Each jar had a different top so they could be easily recognized!

A mummy's guts were kept in jars while the body was mummified.

FAST FACT!

During mummification, the empty body was stuffed with salt so it dried out. This took about 40 days.

A Samurai would rather cut open his own stomach than be defeated.

FAST FACT!

Not only men, but also women and children could become Samurai.

Seppuku, which means "stomach-cutting," was a ritual practiced by Samurai in Japan. The Samurai warrior used a small blade, which he always carried on his body, to stab himself in the stomach if necessary. Samurais chose seppuku when they lost a battle, so that they could die honorably and avoid shame and possible torture by their enemies.

A giant anteater's tongue can flick in and out of its mouth 150 times a minute.

Giant anteaters are the largest species of anteaters and are found throughout much of South and Central America. These creatures are almost blind, but have a great sense of smell so they can sniff out the ants and termites that they live on. Their long, sticky tongue measures around 18 inches long and can be whipped in and out of their mouth as they catch insects. Some giant anteaters can gobble up as many as 30,000 ants and termites in a single day.

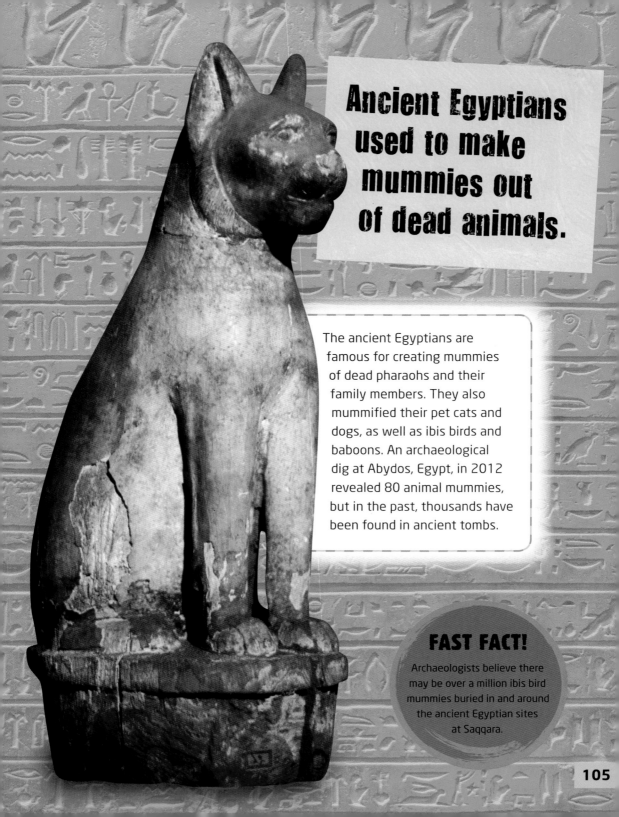

Ancient Egyptians used to make mummies out of dead animals.

The ancient Egyptians are famous for creating mummies of dead pharaohs and their family members. They also mummified their pet cats and dogs, as well as ibis birds and baboons. An archaeological dig at Abydos, Egypt, in 2012 revealed 80 animal mummies, but in the past, thousands have been found in ancient tombs.

FAST FACT!

Archaeologists believe there may be over a million ibis bird mummies buried in and around the ancient Egyptian sites at Saqqara.

An ancient Egyptian king had slaves smeared with honey to attract and catch flies.

Over the centuries, there have been some truly rotten and gross jobs. Slaves and servants have been forced to wipe kings' and queens' bottoms, to empty their toilets, or to check their foods for poison before the rulers sat down for a meal. Pepi II, an ancient Egyptian pharaoh, loathed flies so much that he employed slaves to attract flies so that they stayed away from him.

FAST FACT!

Some modern jobs aren't much fun either. Would you like to be an armpit sniffer for a deodorant company, checking whether new sprays and roll-ons work . . . or not?

Rotting shark meat is served in Iceland as a delicacy called Hákarl.

The people of Iceland catch Greenland sharks, which are then buried in a shallow hole. Heavy stones are placed on top to squeeze the smelly juices out as the shark begins to rot. After 6-10 weeks, the stinky shark is recovered and often served as bite-sized cubes of meat on toothpicks. Be warned—it's a very strong, acidic taste that only a few people can enjoy!

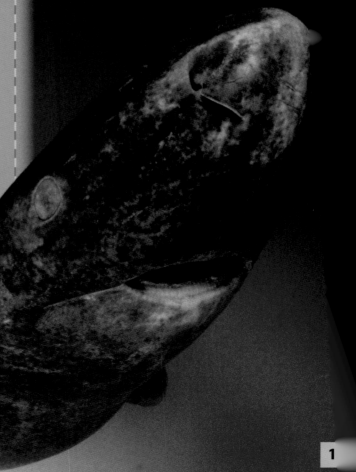

INDEX

Photo Credits

Key: bg = background, m= main image, i = inset, t = top, b = bottom, l = left, r = right f = frame.

Almeda Country Fair: p50m,
Almay: p1bl Picturesbyrob, p19m Peter Horree, P32m Charles Polidano/ Touch The Skies, p48 bg Eye Ubiquitous, p54m Picturebyrob, 55m&i Dinodia Photos, p58i Royalty free images, p63m AlmayCelebrity, p64m Stephen Frink, p65m Adrian Sheratt, p69m AlamyCelebrity, p73m Robert Clayton, p107m GL Archive, p122m INTERFOTO, p127m North Wind Picture Archives, p135m Kathy de Witt, p146m America, p143mt Movie Store Collections, p143mb Medical-on-line, p170 Mim Friday, p172m DK, p182m RIA Novosti, p185m World History Archive, p187m Motoring Picture Library, p188m Beepstock, p195m Paul Wood, p195i PJF News,
Christopher Keleher: p94,
Corbis: p39m Bettman, p183m Michael Maloney/ San Francisco,
Dynamo: p1br Dan Cox, p7m Dan Cox,
FLPA: p20i Mitsuaki Iwago/Minden Pictures, p22m Donald M. Jones/ Minden Pictures, p38m Pete Oxford/Minden Pictures, p61 primrose Peacock, Holt, p77m Stephen Belcher/Minden Pictures, p83m Flip Nicklin/Minden Pictures, p83i Richard Herrmann/Minden Pictures, p94m Andrea Pistolesi, p97m Roland Birke, p99m Library of Congress/ digital version by Science Faction, p100i NBC/Contributor, p101m Topical Press Agency/Stringer, p115m Flip Nicklin/Minden Pictures, p125m Mark Raycroft/Minden pictures, p171m Chris Newbert/Minden Pictures, P192m D P Wilson,
Getty Images: p5m Daniel Berehulak/Staff, p10m Gilbert Carrasquillo/ Contributer, p14m William James Warren, p15m Travel Ink, p16m Patrick McDermott/Contibutor, p17m Science Picture Co, p23m Keystone/Stringer, p25m Bert Morgan/Contributor, p28m Antonio M. Rosario, p29i Jasper Juinen/Staff, p30i SuperStock, p33m Thomas Marent, p34m PhotoQuest/Contributor, p35m Hank Walker/ Contributor, p37m Colin Anderson, p40m Gary Miller/Contributor, p41 Mark Dadswell/Staff, P42m SuperStock, p45m Focus on Sport, p49m Scott Halleran, p52m Time Life pictures, p53m R.J. Eyerman, p56b Photosindia, p60m Silvestre Machado, p71b Ron Sachs, p76m Daniel Simon, p78m Michael Tran, p79m Datacraft Co Ltd, p86m Time Life Pictures/Contributor, p87m Patty Wood/Contributor, p89m Roy Stevens/Contributor, p98m Micheal Ochs Archives/Stringer, p92m Robert NICKELSBERG/Contributor, p102ml Mark Thompson/ Staff, p108m Popperfoto/Contributor,p110m Photoservice Electra, p114m Thomas S. England/Contributor, p117m Michael M. Todaro/ Contributor, p118i Dirck Halstead/Contributor, p128m Francis Miller, p157m David Maclain, p139m Sebastien Bourdon, p129m Rosie Greenway/staff, p147m Ben Stansell, p134m Barcroft Media, p145m Sonny Tumbelaka, p133m Photolibrary, p155m Toa Images Limited, p126m Flickr Open, p158m Paul Redmond, p140m Flickr Open, p131m Flickr, p132m Jeffrey Sylvester, p137m Dan Kitwood, p168m DEA Picture Library/ Contributor, p176m Huey Yoong, p182i Science & Society Picture Library/ contributor, p184m Jonathan Kitchen, p189m New York Daily News Archive/Contributor, p190m Melanie Stetson Freeman/ Contributor, p191m Chris Jackson/Staff, p193bg STEVE GSCHMEISSNER,
NASA: p47m&I, p59m, p119i NASA/JPL-Caltech/Univeristy of Arizona, p82m, p91m, p91i NASA/Bill Ingalls, p96m, p150m, p165m, p173i,
Shutterstock: p1tl Leonello Calvetti, p1r Eric Isselee, p5b Lamella, p5i eldiv, p6b Triff, p6m James Thew, p6i zzoplanet, 8i Qoncept, p9bg Ssergey Kamshylin, p9m pandapaw, p11m Doug Lemke, p11i Ambient Ideas, p12it Georgios Kollidas, p12itf Anusorn P nachol,

p12 im Africa Studio, p12ibgr Guzel, p12ibl Tatiana Popova, p13m Sebastian Kaulitzki, p17bg Sebastian Kaulitzki, p18m Georgi Roshkov, p18i valdis torms, p20b rehoboth foto, p20m Inc, p21b Sinisa Botas, p21m Petrafler, p24m VVK1, p26m Jo Crebbin, p26i Andrew L., p27m kojihirano, p29b Madien, p30bgb James "BO" Insonga, p30mf Poprugin Aleksey, p30i leonello calvetti, p31m DenisNata, p36m dezignor, p33bgb thewhiteview, p33 bgt Piotr Zajc, p39b Alhovik, p40b Cherkas, p40i Helena Esteb, p42i Uryandnikov Sergey, p42bg jarvaman p43m Tami Freed, p44bg mathagraphics, p44i T-Design, p45i Marfot, p45bg Login, p46m Etienne du Preez, p47bg notkoo, p48i Michele Perbellini, p50bg Tamas Gerencser, p51m RimDream, p53bg Alice, p56bg ARENA Creative, p57m Tomasz Szymanski, p58i Peter Waters, p58i Julien Tromeur, p58bg Kuzmin Andrey, p59bg Irina Solatges, p60m Dan Thomas Brostrom, p62m mmaxter, p62bg argus, p64m Antonio Abrignani, p64bg artcasta, p66i Jet Sky, p66bg alterfalter, p67m Ludmilla Yilmaz, p67bg Kororiz Yuriy, p68bg argus, p71bgt Login, p71bgb Irina Solatges, p71m Artsem Martysuik, p72m IDAL, p75m Alita Bobrov, p76bg Vladimir Nitkin, p78i Chichinkin, p78bg Ykh, p80m Zentilia, p85ir Globe Turner, LLC, p88m AlessandroZocc, p90m Anna Hoychuk, p84m Dudarev Mikhail, p85m newphotoservice, p85il Alexander Zavadsky, p92i Rafal Cichawa, p93 m Photo Works, p95m Raywoo, p95i Leonello Calvetti, p100m thieury, p102bg Mario 7, p103m Herbert Kratky, p103bg Lukas Radavicius, p104bg pryzmat, p104m koya979, p105bg GIOck, p105m Eric Isselée, p106m John Kasawa, p109m Luciano Mortula, p111 Grzegorz Wolczyk, p112bg taweesak thiprod, p113m Neale Cousland, p115i Arno van Dulmen/Shutterstock.com, p116m Markus Gann, p118bg edella, p120m Pal Teravagimov, p121m Michael Monahan, p121bg therealtakeone, p123 ArtTomCat, p124m Greg Perry, p129bg LongQuattro, p130bg Subbotina Anna, p130i Nikuwka, p136m Elena Schweitzer, p138bg Nilz, p138i Tovkach Oleg, p138i terekhov igor, p141m Nickolay Stanev, p142bg mitya73, p145m Martin Turzak, p148m Chris Fourie, p151m vectorgirl, p152m Byelikova Oksana, p153m rprongjai, p154m Richard Thorton, p156m Kim Reinick, p157i Le Do, p158bg Robert Adrian Hillman, p159m Eduard Kyslynskyy, p160m Volodymyr Krasyuk, p161m Senol Yaman, p161bg Laborant, p163bg Vector Mushrooms, p164m Dmitrijs Mishejevs, p166m Lefteris Papaulakis, P167 apiguide, p170bg Mario 7, p171i R-O-M-A, p173bg Triff, p173m BW Folsom, p174bg puruan, p174m NinaMalyna, p175m Eric Hui, p175i mary416, p176m Ilya D, Gridnev, p177m atribut, p176bg kentoh, p178bg Everett Collection, p178m Iouri Tcheka/ Shutterstock.com, p179m Anton Balazh, p179i Gillmar, p181m encikat, p186m RedTC, p186i Volker Rauch, p187bg fotomak, p188bg Albachiaraa-, p192i Andy Fox Photography (UK), p193m Heidi Brand, p194bg -Albachiaraa-, p194m Ritu Manoj Jethani, p194i Ritu Manoj Jethani, p195bg PashOK, p196m Herbert Kratky, p196i Cathy Crawford, p197bg chris2766,
SPL: p119m US GEOLOGICAL SURVEY/ SCIENCE PHOTO LIBRARY,